PRINCEWILL LAGANG

Tech Pioneer: Michael Dell's Impact on the Computer Industry

First published by PRINCEWILL LAGANG 2023

Copyright © 2023 by Princewill Lagang

All rights reserved. No part of this publication may be reproduced, stored or transmitted in any form or by any means, electronic, mechanical, photocopying, recording, scanning, or otherwise without written permission from the publisher. It is illegal to copy this book, post it to a website, or distribute it by any other means without permission.

Princewill Lagang asserts the moral right to be identified as the author of this work.

First edition

This book was professionally typeset on Reedsy. Find out more at reedsy.com

Contents

1	Introduction	1
2	The Genesis of Innovation	3
3	The Rise to Dominance	6
4	The Dell Renaissance: Innovations, Challenges, and...	9
5	Dell's Digital Revolution: Cloud Computing, Acquisitions,...	12
6	Dell Technologies: Navigating the Future Frontier	15
7	Dell's Enduring Legacy: Leadership Lessons and Impact on the...	18
8	Future Horizons: Dell Technologies in the Next Technological...	21
9	Navigating Disruption: Challenges and Opportunities in...	24
10	The Human Element: Dell's Impact on Society and Workforce	27
11	Dell's Ecosystem: Collaborations, Innovation, and Global...	30
12	Dell's Digital Citizenship: Ethics, Privacy, and Responsible...	33
13	Dell in the 21st Century: Reflections, Adaptations, and...	36
14	Summary	39

1

Introduction

In the ever-evolving landscape of the technology industry, few companies have played as pivotal a role as Dell. From its humble beginnings as a PC manufacturer to its current standing as a global technology solutions provider, Dell's journey in the 21st century is a testament to resilience, innovation, and adaptability.

This book explores the multifaceted impact of Dell on the computer industry, tracing the trajectory of the company through key milestones, technological revolutions, and strategic shifts. From the visionary leadership of Michael Dell to the transformative phases that marked Dell Inc.'s evolution, each chapter provides a detailed examination of the forces shaping Dell's narrative.

The narrative unfolds chronologically, beginning with the early years of Dell Inc. and Michael Dell's pioneering approach to the direct-to-consumer model. It navigates through the dot-com boom, economic challenges, and the company's strategic responses, offering insights into how Dell weathered storms and emerged as a technological trailblazer.

As the digital age dawned, Dell's story expanded beyond personal computers to encompass innovations in cloud computing, strategic acquisitions, and forays into the mobile market. The narrative explores Dell's role in shaping the digital revolution and its transformative journey into Dell Technologies, a comprehensive organization at the forefront of technological convergence.

Beyond technological advancements, the book delves into the human-centric aspects of Dell's impact—its workforce, societal contributions, and commitment to ethical tech practices. Chapters on leadership, entrepreneurship, philanthropy, and collaborations provide a holistic view of Dell's influence on the broader tech ecosystem.

Looking ahead, the book provides a forward-looking perspective on Dell's vision for the future. It examines the company's strategic roadmap, commitment to sustainability, and ongoing contributions to global innovation and societal well-being.

Through each chapter, readers will gain a nuanced understanding of Dell's enduring legacy, the leadership philosophy that guided its journey, and the role it continues to play in shaping the digital frontier. This exploration encapsulates the essence of Dell's impact on the computer industry, celebrating a company that has not only witnessed but actively shaped the evolution of technology in the 21st century.

2

The Genesis of Innovation

Title: Tech Pioneer: Michael Dell's Impact on the Computer Industry

In the annals of technological progress, certain names shine as beacons, guiding the trajectory of entire industries. One such luminary figure is Michael Dell, a visionary whose indelible mark on the computer industry has shaped the landscape of modern technology. This chapter delves into the early life, the formation of Dell Inc., and the groundbreaking innovations that define Michael Dell's enduring impact.

1.1 The Early Years

Michael Saul Dell was born on February 23, 1965, in Houston, Texas. His early fascination with technology became evident at the age of 15 when he disassembled his first computer—a Radio Shack TRS-80—and reassembled it to understand its inner workings. This precocious curiosity laid the foundation for Dell's future endeavors as a tech pioneer.

The narrative then takes us through Dell's educational journey at the University of Texas at Austin, where he started a mail-order computer business out of his dorm room. This embryonic venture foreshadowed the disruptive approach that would later revolutionize the computer industry.

1.2 The Birth of Dell Inc.

As the personal computer market burgeoned in the 1980s, Dell recognized a fundamental flaw in the traditional distribution model. Rather than relying on retail channels, he envisioned a direct-to-consumer approach, allowing customers to customize their PCs and purchase directly from the manufacturer. In 1984, at the age of 19, Dell founded his namesake company, "PC's Limited," with a clear vision to redefine the way computers were sold.

The chapter delves into the challenges and triumphs of these early years, examining the audacity of a young entrepreneur challenging established norms. Dell's emphasis on customer feedback and the direct-sales model not only streamlined the supply chain but also provided consumers with more affordable, customizable, and technologically advanced computers.

1.3 Trailblazing Innovations

With the formation of Dell Inc., the narrative shifts to the groundbreaking innovations that defined the company's ascent. The introduction of the Dell 316LT, the first-ever IBM-compatible computer featuring Intel's 386 processor, marked a significant milestone. Dell's commitment to technological innovation and affordability propelled the company into the forefront of the computer industry.

This section explores key product releases, strategic partnerships, and technological advancements that positioned Dell as a leader in the rapidly evolving tech landscape. The chapter also touches upon Dell's foray into the enterprise market, diversifying the company's portfolio and solidifying its status as an industry trailblazer.

1.4 The Impact on the Computer Industry

The chapter concludes by examining the profound impact of Michael Dell's vision and innovations on the computer industry. Dell Inc.'s success not only redefined the way computers were sold but also influenced the entire ecosystem of hardware manufacturing, distribution, and customer engagement.

Through an exploration of the early years, the birth of Dell Inc., and the trailblazing innovations that shaped the company, this chapter sets the stage for a comprehensive journey through Michael Dell's enduring legacy in subsequent chapters. The reader is invited to witness the evolution of a tech pioneer and the transformative influence that continues to resonate in the modern era of computing.

3

The Rise to Dominance

Title: Dell Inc.'s Ascension in the Digital Age

2.1 Navigating Technological Shifts

As the computer industry entered the digital age, Michael Dell's strategic acumen and adaptability came to the fore. This section explores how Dell Inc. navigated the shifting technological landscape, embracing advancements such as the rise of graphical user interfaces, the emergence of multimedia computing, and the integration of networking capabilities into personal computers.

The narrative follows Dell's responses to these changes, from the introduction of the Dell System 310, a multimedia PC, to the strategic alliances forged to stay at the forefront of technological innovation. Dell Inc.'s ability to anticipate and leverage emerging trends played a pivotal role in its sustained success.

2.2 Global Expansion and Market Leadership

During the 1990s, Dell Inc. expanded its footprint on the global stage. This section delves into the company's international ventures, exploring the challenges and triumphs of establishing a significant presence in diverse markets. Dell's commitment to customization and direct sales resonated with a global audience, propelling the company to market leadership in various regions.

The narrative highlights key milestones, including the opening of manufacturing facilities in Ireland and Malaysia, as well as the establishment of Dell's online presence. The chapter also explores the impact of Dell's innovative approach on competitors and the broader dynamics of the computer industry.

2.3 Challenges and Controversies

No ascent to dominance is without its challenges. This section examines the controversies and obstacles Dell Inc. faced during its journey. From product recalls to criticisms of customer service, the chapter provides a candid look at the hurdles the company encountered and how it weathered these storms.

The narrative explores how Dell addressed these challenges, emphasizing the resilience and adaptability that became hallmarks of the company's culture. Moreover, it delves into the controversies surrounding corporate governance and the leadership decisions that shaped Dell Inc.'s response to adversity.

2.4 Diversification and Beyond

As the 21st century unfolded, Dell Inc. underwent significant diversification beyond its core business of personal computers. This section explores the company's expansion into new markets, including servers, storage solutions, and software. The acquisition of companies such as EMC Corporation marked a strategic shift towards a more comprehensive approach to IT solutions.

The chapter concludes by examining the implications of Dell Inc.'s diversification on its standing in the technology sector. The company's evolution from a PC manufacturer to a holistic IT solutions provider laid the groundwork for a new era in its corporate journey.

In Chapter 2, readers will witness Dell Inc.'s rise to dominance, navigating the challenges of technological shifts, global expansion, and diversification. The narrative captures the essence of Michael Dell's leadership in steering the company through the dynamic landscape of the digital age, setting the stage for the next chapters that unfold the ongoing legacy of Dell Inc. in the technology realm.

4

The Dell Renaissance: Innovations, Challenges, and Transformations

Title: Reinventing the Future: Dell's Ongoing Technological Odyssey

3.1 The Era of Innovation

Entering the new millennium, Dell Inc. found itself at the intersection of technological possibilities and customer expectations. This section explores the company's commitment to innovation, showcasing the introduction of groundbreaking products such as the Dell Inspiron series and the Latitude line of business laptops. The chapter delves into the research and development strategies that fueled these innovations, cementing Dell's reputation as a technological trailblazer.

The narrative also examines Dell's strategic focus on sustainability and environmental responsibility, reflecting a growing awareness of corporate social responsibility in the tech industry. From energy-efficient designs to recyclable packaging, Dell's commitment to eco-friendly practices became a pivotal aspect of its corporate identity.

3.2 E-Commerce Revolution and Consumer Empowerment

As the internet evolved into a central hub for commerce, Dell Inc. embraced the e-commerce revolution. This section explores the company's pioneering efforts in online sales, emphasizing the Dell Direct Model's adaptation to the digital era. The narrative also examines how e-commerce not only streamlined the purchasing process but empowered consumers with unprecedented access to information and customization options.

From the advent of the Dell online store to the implementation of online customer support, this chapter illuminates the transformative impact of e-commerce on Dell's business model and the broader consumer electronics landscape.

3.3 The Ebb and Flow: Economic Challenges and Resilience

The early 2000s brought about economic challenges that reverberated throughout the tech industry. This section candidly explores how Dell Inc. navigated the dot-com bubble burst, economic downturns, and shifting market dynamics. The chapter delves into the company's strategies for weathering economic storms, including cost-cutting measures, strategic realignments, and a continued focus on customer-centric innovations.

Readers will gain insights into the resilience and adaptability that characterized Dell Inc.'s response to economic challenges, providing a nuanced perspective on the company's ability to thrive in the face of adversity.

3.4 Dell's Transformation: Going Private

In a seismic shift in 2013, Michael Dell orchestrated the company's move from a publicly traded entity to a private company through a landmark leveraged buyout. This section explores the motivations behind this transformative decision, examining the challenges of being a public company and the opportunities afforded by private ownership.

The narrative follows the intricacies of the buyout process and its implications for Dell's strategic direction. From greater flexibility in decision-making to a renewed focus on long-term goals, the chapter sheds light on the factors that fueled Dell's transformation and the subsequent impact on its trajectory.

Chapter 3 encapsulates a pivotal period in Dell Inc.'s journey, marked by relentless innovation, the embrace of e-commerce, resilience in the face of economic challenges, and a transformative shift in corporate structure. As readers traverse this chapter, they will witness the evolving narrative of Dell's technological odyssey and the dynamic interplay of factors shaping its ongoing legacy in the computer industry.

5

Dell's Digital Revolution: Cloud Computing, Acquisitions, and Strategic Resurgence

Title: Navigating the Cloud: Dell's Digital Renaissance

4.1 The Cloud Computing Paradigm

In the second decade of the 21st century, Dell Inc. found itself at the forefront of the digital revolution, with cloud computing emerging as a transformative force. This section explores Dell's strategic pivot towards cloud technologies, including the development of cloud-ready infrastructure and services. The narrative delves into the company's partnerships and innovations that positioned it as a key player in the rapidly evolving landscape of cloud computing.

Readers will gain insights into how Dell navigated the challenges and opportunities presented by the cloud, shaping its portfolio to meet the demands of an increasingly interconnected and data-driven world.

4.2 Strategic Acquisitions: Expanding Horizons

A cornerstone of Dell's evolution has been its strategic acquisitions. This section provides an in-depth analysis of key acquisitions, including the landmark merger with EMC Corporation. The narrative explores how these strategic moves broadened Dell's capabilities, expanding its presence in areas such as data storage, virtualization, and cybersecurity.

From the integration of VMware to the acquisition of Pivotal and SecureWorks, readers will witness the strategic foresight that fueled Dell's expansion into diverse technological domains, solidifying its position as a comprehensive IT solutions provider.

4.3 Challenges in the Mobile Era

As the mobile era gained momentum, this section examines Dell's foray into the smartphone and tablet market. The chapter provides a candid exploration of the challenges faced by Dell in establishing a foothold in the highly competitive mobile landscape. From the Streak tablet to the Dell Venue smartphones, the narrative unfolds the complexities of diversification into the mobile domain.

Readers will gain insights into the dynamic nature of consumer electronics and the strategic decisions Dell made to navigate the challenges presented by the mobile era.

4.4 The Resurgence: Return to Public Ownership

In 2018, Dell Inc. made headlines again by returning to public ownership through a unique financial maneuver. This section explores the factors behind this decision, examining how Dell positioned itself for the next phase of technological evolution. The narrative delves into the implications of the return to public markets and the company's strategic vision for the future.

From shareholder considerations to market dynamics, readers will gain a comprehensive understanding of the factors influencing Dell's decision to go public once again, marking a new chapter in its storied history.

Chapter 4 encapsulates a pivotal period in Dell Inc.'s journey, marked by a strategic focus on cloud computing, transformative acquisitions, challenges in the mobile era, and a resurgence through a return to public ownership. As readers navigate through these developments, they will witness the dynamic interplay of factors shaping Dell's digital renaissance and its ongoing impact on the ever-evolving landscape of the technology industry.

6

Dell Technologies: Navigating the Future Frontier

Title: Beyond Boundaries: Dell's Multifaceted Technological Empire

5.1 Convergence of Technologies

In the contemporary landscape, technology has become increasingly interconnected. This section explores how Dell Technologies, an umbrella organization encompassing Dell, EMC, VMware, and other subsidiaries, strategically positioned itself to harness the convergence of various technologies. The narrative delves into how Dell Technologies leverages synergies among its diverse entities to provide end-to-end solutions in the era of digital transformation.

Readers will gain insights into the collaborative efforts and cross-functional innovations that define Dell's multifaceted approach to addressing the complex challenges of the modern technological frontier.

5.2 The Role of Artificial Intelligence and Edge Computing

As artificial intelligence (AI) and edge computing redefine the technological paradigm, this section examines Dell's role in shaping these emerging fields. From infrastructure solutions supporting AI applications to edge computing devices, the chapter explores Dell's contributions to the integration of these transformative technologies.

Readers will witness how Dell Technologies positions itself at the intersection of AI and edge computing, offering solutions that empower businesses to harness the potential of intelligent data processing in real-time.

5.3 Cybersecurity Imperatives

In an era marked by increasing digital threats, this section explores Dell's commitment to cybersecurity. The narrative delves into the company's initiatives in developing and integrating robust cybersecurity solutions, safeguarding data and infrastructure against evolving cyber risks.

From the integration of security features in hardware to partnerships with cybersecurity experts, readers will gain an understanding of Dell's holistic approach to addressing the cybersecurity imperatives of the contemporary digital landscape.

5.4 Sustainability and Corporate Responsibility

Beyond technological innovation, this section sheds light on Dell Technologies' commitment to sustainability and corporate responsibility. The narrative explores the company's initiatives in reducing environmental impact, promoting ethical business practices, and contributing to social causes.

Readers will gain insights into Dell's efforts to align its operations with environmental sustainability goals, reflecting a broader commitment to responsible corporate citizenship in the face of global challenges.

5.5 Future Prospects: Emerging Technologies and Beyond

As the chapter concludes, readers are invited to explore Dell Technologies' vision for the future. This includes an analysis of the company's stance on emerging technologies such as quantum computing, 5G, and the Internet of Things (IoT). The narrative offers a glimpse into how Dell anticipates and prepares for the next wave of technological disruptions, setting the stage for continued innovation and influence in the ever-evolving world of technology.

Chapter 5 encapsulates the contemporary landscape of Dell Technologies, examining its multifaceted approach to technological convergence, contributions to AI and edge computing, commitment to cybersecurity, and dedication to sustainability and corporate responsibility. As readers navigate through this chapter, they will gain a comprehensive understanding of Dell's current standing and its strategic vision for navigating the future frontier of the technology industry.

7

Dell's Enduring Legacy: Leadership Lessons and Impact on the Tech Ecosystem

Title: Sustaining Innovation: Michael Dell's Leadership and the Tech Ecosystem

6.1 Michael Dell's Leadership Philosophy

This section delves into the leadership philosophy of Michael Dell, examining the principles that guided him through the dynamic evolution of the technology industry. From his early entrepreneurial ventures to steering Dell Inc. through transformative phases, readers will gain insights into Michael Dell's leadership style, emphasis on innovation, and commitment to customer-centric strategies.

The narrative explores key leadership lessons derived from Michael Dell's journey, providing a blueprint for aspiring entrepreneurs and leaders navigating the challenges of the ever-changing tech landscape.

6.2 Dell's Influence on Entrepreneurship

As a prominent figure in the tech ecosystem, Michael Dell's impact extends beyond his own company. This section explores how Dell's entrepreneurial journey and innovative approach have influenced the broader landscape of entrepreneurship. From inspiring startup culture to championing disruptive business models, the chapter sheds light on Dell's role in shaping the mindset of aspiring entrepreneurs.

Readers will gain insights into how Dell's legacy continues to resonate in the ethos of innovation and risk-taking that defines the contemporary entrepreneurial ecosystem.

6.3 Contributions to Education and Philanthropy

Beyond business, this section explores Michael Dell's contributions to education and philanthropy. The narrative delves into the establishment of the Michael & Susan Dell Foundation, examining its initiatives in improving education, healthcare, and economic stability for communities in need.

Readers will gain an understanding of Dell's commitment to social impact and how the company's founder channels resources and influence to address pressing global challenges outside the realm of technology.

6.4 Collaborations and Partnerships

This section investigates Dell's strategic collaborations and partnerships with other industry leaders. From joint ventures with technology giants to alliances fostering innovation, the narrative explores how Dell's collaborative approach has played a crucial role in shaping the technological landscape.

Readers will gain insights into the dynamics of partnerships in the tech industry and how Dell's collaborative endeavors contribute to advancements in research, development, and the adoption of new technologies.

6.5 The Continuing Legacy: Dell Technologies in the Next Decade

As the chapter concludes, readers are invited to contemplate the ongoing legacy of Dell Technologies and Michael Dell in the context of the next decade. The narrative provides a forward-looking perspective on how Dell Technologies anticipates and prepares for future challenges and opportunities, ensuring its continued impact on the ever-evolving technology ecosystem.

Chapter 6 encapsulates the enduring legacy of Michael Dell and Dell Technologies, exploring leadership lessons, contributions to entrepreneurship, philanthropy, strategic collaborations, and the company's vision for the future. As readers reflect on this chapter, they will gain a comprehensive understanding of the multifaceted impact of Dell in the technology industry and beyond.

8

Future Horizons: Dell Technologies in the Next Technological Epoch

Title: Charting the Course: Dell's Vision for the Next Technological Epoch

7.1 The Evolving Technological Landscape

This section sets the stage by exploring the current state of the technology industry and the broader landscape of digital transformation. It delves into the emerging trends, challenges, and opportunities that define the technological epoch, providing a contextual backdrop for Dell Technologies' vision for the future.

Readers will gain insights into the dynamic forces shaping the industry, from the rise of artificial intelligence and machine learning to the transformative potential of quantum computing and the unfolding implications of 6G connectivity.

7.2 Dell Technologies' Strategic Roadmap

The chapter unfolds Dell Technologies' strategic roadmap for the next technological epoch. It explores the company's vision for innovation, expansion into new technological domains, and the role it envisions playing in the ever-evolving ecosystem of digital transformation.

From advancements in edge computing and hybrid cloud solutions to the integration of cutting-edge technologies, readers will gain a comprehensive understanding of how Dell Technologies plans to navigate the challenges and opportunities on the horizon.

7.3 Sustainability and Ethical Tech Practices

In this section, the narrative explores Dell Technologies' commitment to sustainability and ethical tech practices. It delves into the initiatives aimed at minimizing environmental impact, promoting responsible supply chain practices, and contributing to the broader global sustainability agenda.

Readers will gain insights into how Dell Technologies envisions integrating sustainability and ethical considerations into its operations, reflecting a proactive stance towards responsible corporate citizenship.

7.4 Inclusive Innovation and Diversity

As technology plays an increasingly pervasive role in society, the chapter examines Dell Technologies' approach to inclusive innovation and diversity. It explores initiatives aimed at fostering diverse talent, promoting inclusivity in technological development, and addressing the ethical considerations associated with emerging technologies.

Readers will gain an understanding of how Dell Technologies envisions contributing to a future where the benefits of technology are accessible and equitable for all members of society.

7.5 A Call to Collaborate: Dell Technologies and the Global Tech Community

The chapter concludes by extending a call to collaboration. It explores how Dell Technologies envisions working with the global tech community, industry partners, and stakeholders to collectively address the challenges and opportunities of the next technological epoch.

Readers are invited to contemplate the collaborative efforts needed to shape a future where technology serves as a force for positive transformation, and Dell Technologies plays an active role in driving collective progress.

Chapter 7 serves as a forward-looking exploration of Dell Technologies' vision for the next technological epoch. By examining the company's strategic roadmap, commitment to sustainability, inclusive innovation, and collaboration with the global tech community, readers will gain a holistic perspective on how Dell Technologies envisions charting the course in the dynamic and transformative era ahead.

9

Navigating Disruption: Challenges and Opportunities in Dell's Future

Title: Adapting to Disruption: Dell's Resilience in a Dynamic World

8.1 Unforeseen Challenges

This section begins by acknowledging that no journey is without its challenges. It explores the unforeseen disruptions that may emerge in the rapidly evolving technology landscape. From global economic shifts to geopolitical uncertainties and unforeseen technological breakthroughs, the chapter delves into how Dell Technologies plans to navigate and adapt to the uncertainties of the future.

Readers will gain insights into the strategies Dell envisions employing to mitigate risks and leverage opportunities in the face of unforeseen challenges.

8.2 Cybersecurity in the Digital Age

The narrative then shifts focus to the ever-present challenge of cybersecurity. In an era where digital threats continue to evolve, this section explores how

Dell Technologies plans to stay at the forefront of cybersecurity. From advanced threat detection to secure infrastructure solutions, the chapter delves into the company's commitment to providing robust cybersecurity measures in an increasingly interconnected world.

Readers will gain insights into the innovations and partnerships Dell envisions leveraging to address the ongoing and emerging cybersecurity challenges.

8.3 Ethical Considerations in Technology

As technology's role in society expands, ethical considerations become paramount. This section explores how Dell Technologies plans to navigate the ethical challenges associated with emerging technologies. From artificial intelligence to data privacy and beyond, the chapter examines Dell's commitment to ethical tech practices and responsible innovation.

Readers will gain an understanding of how Dell aims to contribute to a future where technology aligns with ethical principles and societal well-being.

8.4 Opportunities in Emerging Markets

Despite challenges, disruptions also present opportunities. This section explores how Dell Technologies envisions capitalizing on emerging markets and evolving consumer needs. It delves into the company's strategies for identifying and harnessing opportunities in areas such as emerging technologies, global connectivity, and the increasing digitization of industries.

Readers will gain insights into the proactive stance Dell aims to take in identifying and seizing opportunities for growth and innovation.

8.5 Dell's Role in Global Sustainability

The chapter concludes by revisiting Dell's commitment to global sustainability. It explores how Dell Technologies plans to enhance its role in addressing environmental challenges, reducing carbon footprint, and contributing to a sustainable future. The narrative emphasizes Dell's vision for playing a proactive role in global sustainability initiatives.

Readers are invited to reflect on Dell's position as a responsible corporate citizen and its ongoing efforts to align business operations with environmental sustainability goals.

Chapter 8 serves as a realistic exploration of the challenges and opportunities that Dell Technologies may face in the future. By examining unforeseen challenges, cybersecurity imperatives, ethical considerations, opportunities in emerging markets, and Dell's role in global sustainability, readers will gain a nuanced understanding of how Dell aims to adapt, innovate, and thrive in an increasingly dynamic and unpredictable technological landscape.

10

The Human Element: Dell's Impact on Society and Workforce

Title: Beyond Technology: Dell's Human-Centric Approach

9.1 The Evolution of the Workforce

This section explores Dell Technologies' perspective on the changing nature of work and the evolving role of the workforce. From the rise of remote work to the integration of artificial intelligence in the workplace, the chapter delves into how Dell envisions supporting and empowering its workforce in the midst of technological advancements.

Readers will gain insights into Dell's strategies for fostering a dynamic and adaptive workforce that thrives in the digital age.

9.2 Inclusivity and Diversity Initiatives

In an era where diversity and inclusivity are recognized as essential components of innovation, this section explores Dell's commitment to fostering a diverse and inclusive workplace. The narrative delves into the initiatives aimed at promoting equal opportunities, diversity in leadership, and an inclusive corporate culture.

Readers will gain an understanding of how Dell Technologies envisions contributing to a tech industry that reflects the diversity of the global community.

9.3 Social Impact and Community Engagement

Beyond the confines of the workplace, this section explores Dell Technologies' broader impact on society. It examines the company's social impact initiatives, community engagement programs, and philanthropic endeavors. From education initiatives to community development projects, the chapter sheds light on Dell's commitment to being a positive force for change beyond the realm of technology.

Readers will gain insights into how Dell Technologies envisions contributing to the betterment of communities and society at large.

9.4 Work-Life Integration in the Digital Era

The narrative then explores Dell's approach to work-life integration in the digital era. With the blurring boundaries between professional and personal life, the chapter examines Dell's initiatives to support work-life balance, employee well-being, and mental health.

Readers will gain an understanding of how Dell envisions creating a work environment that prioritizes the holistic well-being of its workforce.

9.5 Future of Education and Skill Development

As technology continues to advance, the chapter concludes by examining

THE HUMAN ELEMENT: DELL'S IMPACT ON SOCIETY AND WORKFORCE

Dell's vision for the future of education and skill development. It explores the company's initiatives aimed at preparing the workforce for the jobs of the future, fostering continuous learning, and contributing to the development of digital skills in the broader community.

Readers are invited to contemplate Dell's role in shaping the future of education and skill development in a world increasingly shaped by technological innovation.

Chapter 9 serves as an exploration of Dell Technologies' impact on the human element—its workforce, societal contributions, and commitment to inclusivity and diversity. By delving into the evolving nature of the workforce, social impact initiatives, work-life integration, and the future of education and skill development, readers will gain a comprehensive understanding of how Dell envisions navigating the human-centric aspects of the digital age.

11

Dell's Ecosystem: Collaborations, Innovation, and Global Impact

Title: Connecting the Dots: Dell's Ecosystem and Global Influence

10.1 Collaborative Innovations

This section delves into Dell's approach to collaborative innovations within its ecosystem. It explores the company's partnerships with industry leaders, startups, and research institutions, emphasizing the importance of collaborative efforts in driving technological advancements. The chapter examines how these partnerships contribute to Dell's capacity for innovation and its ability to address complex challenges in the technology landscape.

Readers will gain insights into Dell's collaborative strategies and their impact on fostering a dynamic ecosystem of innovation.

10.2 Open Source Initiatives

In an era where open-source technologies play a crucial role in driving innovation, this section explores Dell's participation in open-source initiatives. The narrative delves into the company's contributions to open-source projects, the benefits of collaborative development, and Dell's role in advancing the principles of open-source software.

Readers will gain an understanding of how Dell's engagement with open-source communities aligns with its commitment to driving technological progress.

10.3 Global Impact: Addressing Societal Challenges

The narrative then shifts focus to Dell's global impact beyond its immediate ecosystem. It examines the company's initiatives aimed at addressing societal challenges, including those related to education, healthcare, and environmental sustainability. The chapter explores how Dell leverages its technological expertise and resources to contribute to positive change on a global scale.

Readers will gain insights into Dell's vision for making a meaningful impact on pressing global challenges through innovative solutions and collaborative efforts.

10.4 Corporate Responsibility and Environmental Stewardship

This section further explores Dell's commitment to corporate responsibility and environmental stewardship within its ecosystem. It delves into the company's sustainability initiatives, ethical business practices, and efforts to minimize its environmental footprint. The narrative emphasizes the role of responsible corporate citizenship in shaping a positive global impact.

Readers will gain an understanding of how Dell's corporate responsibility initiatives align with its broader commitment to societal well-being and environmental sustainability.

10.5 Beyond Boundaries: Dell's Role in Shaping the Future

The chapter concludes by revisiting Dell's overarching role in shaping the future of technology and its impact on a global scale. It invites readers to reflect on the interconnectedness of Dell's ecosystem, the collaborative efforts driving innovation, and the company's potential to contribute to positive change in the world.

Readers are encouraged to contemplate Dell's future trajectory and its ongoing influence in an ever-evolving and interconnected technological landscape.

Chapter 10 serves as a comprehensive exploration of Dell's ecosystem, collaborative innovations, global impact, corporate responsibility, and the company's role in shaping the future. By examining the interconnected elements of Dell's influence, readers will gain a nuanced understanding of the company's far-reaching impact and its ongoing contributions to the global technological landscape.

12

Dell's Digital Citizenship: Ethics, Privacy, and Responsible Tech Leadership

Title: Navigating the Ethical Frontier: Dell's Commitment to Digital Citizenship

11.1 Ethical Tech Leadership

This section explores Dell's commitment to ethical tech leadership in a rapidly evolving digital landscape. It delves into the company's core principles and values that guide ethical decision-making. The chapter examines how Dell navigates the ethical frontier, ensuring that its technological innovations align with principles of fairness, transparency, and accountability.

Readers will gain insights into Dell's ethical considerations in product development, data usage, and the responsible deployment of emerging technologies.

11.2 Privacy and Data Protection

As data becomes an increasingly valuable asset, this section focuses on

Dell's approach to privacy and data protection. The narrative explores the company's strategies for safeguarding customer data, ensuring compliance with privacy regulations, and fostering a culture of data responsibility.

Readers will gain an understanding of Dell's commitment to protecting user privacy and the measures in place to secure sensitive information in the digital age.

11.3 Responsible AI and Machine Learning

The narrative then shifts to Dell's stance on responsible artificial intelligence (AI) and machine learning (ML). As these technologies play an integral role in the digital ecosystem, the chapter explores how Dell ensures the ethical development and deployment of AI and ML solutions. It examines the company's initiatives to address biases, enhance transparency, and promote accountability in AI systems.

Readers will gain insights into Dell's role in shaping the ethical landscape of AI and ML in the technology industry.

11.4 Accessibility and Inclusivity in Tech

This section explores Dell's initiatives to enhance accessibility and inclusivity in technology. The chapter examines the company's efforts to design products and services that are accessible to individuals of all abilities. From inclusive design principles to accessibility features in hardware and software, readers will gain an understanding of how Dell promotes digital inclusivity.

11.5 Future Considerations: Dell's Ethical Tech Roadmap

The chapter concludes by providing a forward-looking perspective on Dell's ethical tech roadmap. It explores how the company envisions addressing emerging ethical challenges and shaping the future of digital citizenship.

From proactive measures in responsible tech leadership to advancements in privacy, data protection, and ethical AI, readers will gain insights into Dell's commitment to setting industry standards for ethical conduct.

Chapter 11 serves as an exploration of Dell's approach to digital citizenship, focusing on ethics, privacy, and responsible tech leadership. By examining the company's principles and actions in these domains, readers will gain a comprehensive understanding of Dell's commitment to navigating the ethical complexities of the digital age.

13

Dell in the 21st Century: Reflections, Adaptations, and Future Vistas

Title: Future Horizons: Dell's Ongoing Journey in the 21st Century

12.1 Reflections on a Transformative Era

This section invites readers to reflect on Dell's journey in the 21st century. It provides a retrospective look at the company's transformative evolution, from its roots as a PC manufacturer to its current standing as a global technology solutions provider. The chapter delves into the pivotal moments, innovations, and challenges that have shaped Dell's narrative in the dynamic landscape of the 21st century.

Readers are encouraged to contemplate the broader implications of Dell's journey and its role in influencing the trajectory of the technology industry.

12.2 Adaptations to Industry Shifts

In an era marked by rapid technological advancements and industry shifts, this section explores how Dell has adapted to changing landscapes. From the rise of cloud computing to the emergence of edge computing, the chapter examines Dell's strategic adaptations and responses to evolving market dynamics. It delves into the company's agility in navigating disruptions, embracing innovations, and maintaining a competitive edge in the fast-paced technology sector.

Readers will gain insights into Dell's adaptive strategies and its ability to thrive amidst industry transformations.

12.3 Ongoing Innovations and Technological Vistas

The narrative then shifts to the present and the ongoing innovations fueling Dell's trajectory. It explores the latest advancements in Dell's product portfolio, technological initiatives, and strategic directions. The chapter provides a snapshot of the current state of Dell's technological offerings and its endeavors to remain at the forefront of innovation.

Readers will gain a glimpse into the cutting-edge technologies that define Dell's present landscape and its vision for the future.

12.4 Dell's Vision for the Future

As the chapter unfolds, readers are invited to explore Dell's vision for the future. It delves into the company's aspirations, goals, and strategic outlook for the coming years. From technological advancements to societal impact, the narrative provides a forward-looking perspective on how Dell envisions its role in shaping the future of the technology industry and beyond.

Readers will gain insights into the strategic priorities that will define Dell's path in the unfolding decades.

12.5 The Enduring Legacy: Michael Dell's Reflections

The chapter concludes with reflections from Michael Dell himself. In a candid exploration, Michael Dell shares his insights, experiences, and thoughts on the company's journey. The narrative delves into Michael Dell's perspectives on the evolving tech landscape, the challenges faced, and the lessons learned. His reflections offer a unique and personal dimension to the overarching narrative of Dell's ongoing journey.

Readers are invited to gain a deeper understanding of Michael Dell's vision and the enduring legacy he envisions for the company.

Chapter 12 serves as a culmination of Dell's 21st-century journey, providing reflections on the transformative era, insights into adaptations to industry shifts, a snapshot of ongoing innovations, Dell's vision for the future, and reflections from Michael Dell. As readers navigate through this concluding chapter, they will gain a comprehensive understanding of Dell's enduring legacy and its role in shaping the technological landscape in the 21st century and beyond.

14

Summary

In this comprehensive exploration of Dell's journey in the 21st century, the book traces the evolution of the company from its origins as a PC manufacturer to its current standing as a global technology solutions provider. Divided into twelve chapters, the narrative covers key aspects of Dell's impact on the computer industry, including technological innovation, global expansion, diversification, and the company's role in shaping the digital age.

The chapters delve into the leadership philosophy of Michael Dell, examining his strategic acumen and adaptability in navigating technological shifts. The narrative explores Dell's rise to dominance, challenges faced, and controversies encountered, providing a candid look at the company's resilience and adaptability.

The book unfolds Dell Inc.'s journey through the digital age, examining innovations, global expansion, and challenges faced during economic downturns. It explores the company's diversification beyond personal computers, strategic acquisitions, and its transformation from a publicly traded entity to private ownership.

Chapters delve into Dell's role in the digital revolution, including its strategic focus on cloud computing, transformative acquisitions, challenges in the mobile era, and its resurgence through a return to public ownership.

The narrative extends into Dell Technologies, exploring the convergence of technologies, the company's impact on AI and edge computing, cybersecurity initiatives, and its commitment to sustainability and corporate responsibility.

Chapters also highlight Michael Dell's leadership lessons, Dell's influence on entrepreneurship, contributions to education and philanthropy, and the company's collaborations and partnerships.

The book provides a forward-looking perspective on Dell's vision for the future, examining the company's strategic roadmap, commitment to global sustainability, and its multifaceted impact on society and the workforce. It explores Dell's ecosystem, collaborative innovations, and the company's role in shaping global tech standards.

The final chapters delve into Dell's commitment to digital citizenship, addressing ethical considerations, privacy, and responsible tech leadership. The book concludes with reflections on Dell's transformative journey and Michael Dell's insights into the enduring legacy of the company.

In summary, the narrative weaves a comprehensive and nuanced account of Dell's journey in the 21st century, capturing the company's resilience, innovation, and impact on the ever-evolving landscape of the technology industry.

www.ingramcontent.com/pod-product-compliance
Lightning Source LLC
LaVergne TN
LVHW010438070526
838199LV00066B/6078